POCAHONTAS AND HER TWO HUSBANDS

The TRUTH, Not Animated Fiction, About Her Marriages to Kocoum and John Rolfe (Not John Smith)

By

John L. Rolfe

POCAHONTAS AND HER TWO HUSBANDS#

Copyright © 2017 by John L. Rolfe

All rights reserved. No part of this book may be used or reproduced by any means, graphic, electronic, digital, or mechanical, including photocopying, recording, taping, or by any information storage retrieval system, without the express written permission of the copyright holder except in the case of brief quotations embodies in critical articles or reviews.

The views expressed in this work are solely those of the author and do not necessarily reflect the views of the publisher.

ISBN-13: 978-1544818191
ISBN-10: 154481819x

Ambassador Family Press
West Chester, PA

Table of Contents

Chapter 1: Animated Fiction, the Disney Pocahontas Films

Chapter 2: Pocahontas' Early Life

Chapter 3: Pocahontas Had Her First Contact with the English When She Was Age 10

Chapter 4: Pocahontas Married Indian Warrior Kocoum When She Was Age 12

Chapter 5: When She Was Age 15, Pocahontas Was Kidnapped and Her Husband Kocoum Was Killed by English Captain Samuel Argall

Chapter 6: Pocahontas Married John Rolfe When She Was Age 16 and Began the *Peace of Pocahontas*

Chapter 7: Pocahontas' Life with John Rolfe, Her English Virginia Settler Husband

Chapter 8: Pocahontas Became the Toast of London When She Was Age 18

Chapter 9: Pocahontas Died When She Was Age 19

Appendix: John Rolfe's Letter of March 1614 to Sir Thomas Dale, Governor of Virginia, Seeking Permission to Marry Pocahontas

Other Books by John L. Rolfe

About the Author

Chapter 1: ANIMATED FICTION, THE DISNEY POCAHONTAS FILMS

DISNEY'S ANIMATED FILMS WITH GENUINE HISTORIC NAMES BUT FICTIONAL STORIES MISLED GENERATIONS OF AMERICANS

The animated films *Pocahontas* (1995) and *Pocahontas II* (1998) by Walt Disney Pictures did a huge disservice to several generations of Americans. In the interests of a good story – Disney never claimed these films were documentaries – Disney fictionalized or made up many, many things and changed many of the historical facts we do know. This misled not only the children – shame on you Disney – but also the parents who saw the animated films with their children.

POCAHONTAS WAS A CHILD OF 10 WHEN SHE MET JOHN SMITH

May 1608 was Pocahontas' first visit to the fort at Jamestown. It was her first known contact with the English and with John Smith. She was 10 years old at the time, having been born on September 17, 1597. She was not a mature teenager as depicted in the animated film Pocahontas.

John Smith described first seeing Pocahontas in May 1608 in his letter of June 2, 1608, which was later published as *A True Relation of Such Occurrences and Accidents of Note as Have Happened in Virginia Since the First Planting of That Colony Which Is Now Resident in the South Part Thereof, Till the Last Return.*

This is what happened. In April 1608, Smith captured seven Paspaheghan Indians as a result of a trade disagreement. The Paspaheghans were one of about 31 tribes in the Powhatan confederacy. Chief Powhatan's response was to send a diplomatic envoy to secure the release of the captured Paspaheghans.

Smith first mentioned Pocahontas in this June 2, 1608 letter as part of Powhatan's response to Smith's capture of the seven Paspaheghans in April 1608. Smith relates that in May 1608, Chief Powhatan sent his daughter Pocahontas and a man named Rawhunt as diplomatic envoys to secure the release of the Paspaheghans held by the colonists. John Smith even described Pocahontas in his June 1608 letter:

Powhatan ... sent his Daughter, a child of ten years old, which not only for feature, countenance, and proportion much exceedeth any of the rest of his people, but for wit and spirit the only Nonpareil of his Country. This he sent by his most trusty messenger, called Rawhunt ...

This was Smith's first mention of Chief Powhatan's daughter Pocahontas.

Also, in Smith's 1612 book about his Virginia adventure, he made no mention of meeting Pocahontas before May 1608.

POCAHNOTAS DID NOT RESCUE JOHN SMITH

Historians generally agree that Smith's story of rescue by Pocahontas is not true. Notably, Native American sources all say it is not true. Further, in personal conversations with traditional Native Americans, the author has been informed that a child would never be present at an event such as described by Smith.

This story of Smith's purported rescue occurred more than four months before Smith, by his own admission, first met Pocahontas.

It is true that Smith was captured in December 1607 by paramount Chief Powhatan's brother Chief Opechancanough, the werowance, or chief of the Pamunkey tribe, after a battle in which several men were killed. Smith was freed and returned to Jamestown on January 2, 1608.

Smith did not mention being threatened with clubs or rescued by Pocahontas in his June 2, 1608 letter.

Smith also made no mention of being threatened with clubs or rescued by Pocahontas during his December 1607 capture in his 1612 book about his Virginia adventure, *The Proceedings of the English Colony in Virginia Since Their First Beginning From England in the Year of Our Lord 1606, Till This Present 1612, With All Their Accidents That Befell Them in Their Journeys and Discoveries.*

Additionally, Smith made no mention of being threatened with clubs or rescued by Pocahontas during his December 1607 capture when Pocahontas visited England in 1616.

John Smith first related the story of his purported rescue in December 1607 by Pocahontas for the first and only time in his 1624 book, 16 years later. By that time, everyone else purportedly involved was dead and could not refute what he said.

Although the purported rescue story is false, Pocahontas had become a celebrity in London in 1617 and Smith's dramatic rescue story could have helped the sales of Smith's book. As the story was repeated over the next 400 years, it likely increased the sales of books and films, including the Disney animated films, which included the false story.

POCAHONTAS DID NOT FALL IN LOVE WITH JOHN SMITH

This is pure Disney fiction to tell a simpler story.

POCAHONTAS DID NOT MARRY JOHN SMITH

The Disney film Pocahontas doesn't actually say Pocahontas married John Smith, but the false love story and the ambiguous ending have led many to believe that they did marry, and others to believe they should have married.

THE AGE OF KOCOUM

The Disney animated film shows Kocoum as a quite mature man, while history records him as being a young and vigorous warrior.

POCAHONTAS' LOVE FOR KOCOUM

Kocoum was a warrior and one of Chief Powhatan's personal guards. The line in the Disney animated film when Pocahontas said her destiny lay in another direction, meaning John Smith, when her father the paramount Chief Powhatan approved her marriage to the warrior Kocoum, is pure fiction. Pocahontas not only married Kocoum, but also as far as history knows, Pocahontas had a conventional loving marriage with Kocoum.

POCAHONTAS II, JOHN ROLFE VS. JOHN RATCLIFFE

The John Rolfe vs. John Ratcliffe rivalry which runs throughout the Pocahontas II animated film, starting in Virginia and continuing later in England, is totally false. John Rolfe and John Ratcliffe were not in Virginia at the same time. And Ratcliffe died before John Rolfe first arrived in Virginia. There is also no evidence that John

Rolfe and John Ratcliffe knew each other in England before either went to Virginia.

John Ratcliffe went to Jamestown as Captain of the smallest of the original three ships, the Discovery. He left London on December 20, 1606, arrived on the Virginia coast on April 26, 1607, and finally reached in Jamestown on May 14, 1607. At that time, Edward Maria Wingfield was elected President of the Council of Virginia. On September 10, 1607, Wingfield was removed by the other Council members and John Ratcliffe was elected President of the Council. A year later, on September 10, 1608, when his one year term as President of the Council expired, he was succeeded by Captain John Smith as President of the Council. Ratcliffe sailed back to England in January 1609 and returned to Virginia in June 1609. In early 1610 Ratcliffe and others went on a trading expedition with the Powhatan and Ratcliffe and most of the others were killed in an ambush. This happened before John Rolfe first arrived in Jamestown on May 23, 1610.

Thus, a rivalry between Rolfe and Ratcliffe in Virginia and later in England was impossible.

HISTORY, NOT ANIMATED FICTION

The rest of this book will be about the actual history, not animated fiction, of Pocahontas and her two husbands, Kocoum and John Rolfe.

Chapter 2: POCAHONTAS' EARLY LIFE

THE BEST OF TIMES, THE WORST OF TIMES

Starting with the day she was born and continuing through her brief but very important and influential life, it would be the best of times and the worst of times for the Powhatan Indian woman we know as Pocahontas.

It was the worst of times for Pocahontas in many ways. Her very entry into the world was marred by tragedy, the death of her mother giving birth to her.

Again at age 15 tragedy struck her three times, when in one day she was kidnapped by the English Captain Samuel Argall, her first husband Kocoum was murdered by the English, and she saw her first child, Little Kocoum, for the last time.

Finally, tragedy struck a final time when she died, probably of disease, across the ocean in England far from her home, at 19 years of age.

It was the best of times for Pocahontas as she had a carefree childhood, a father who loved her deeply, and an older sister who raised her and who also loved her greatly.

It was the best of times when she had a child with each of her two husbands and those children lived and produced many descendants. Pocahontas was even philosophical about her death on March 21, 1617. John Rolfe wrote in a letter of June 8, 1617, after his return to Virginia following the death of Pocahontas, that Pocahontas said on her deathbed that all must die but it is enough that her child lives.

At least from the English perspective, it was the best of times because Pocahontas was largely responsible for the success of the English in America years before the first Massachusetts colony was established in 1620.

Also, Pocahontas' marriage to the settler and planter John Rolfe, the first interracial church marriage in what would become the United States of America, and the resulting *Peace of Pocahontas*, stopped the war with the Indians that the English were losing, and allowed the English to get enough settlers in Virginia so that they could not be eliminated.

Further, although John Rolfe was the first successful planter of tobacco, America's First Entrepreneur, the mentoring he received from relatives of Pocahontas, possibly her uncle

Uttamattamakin, helped him cure the tobacco in a better way and make his tobacco even more successful. John Rolfe's successful cultivation of tobacco caused Virginia to be a financial success and continue as the first permanent English colony in America, when the sponsors of the colony, the Virginia Company of London, until then had been considering abandoning the colony for its failure to produce any profit.

The extraordinary accomplishments of Pocahontas in a life of 19 years were the best of times! Pocahontas was without a doubt the most important woman in Colonial America.

Pocahontas may also have been the most important woman in American history. In fact, there might not have been any American history as we know it, of a successful English colony and later an independent English-speaking United States of America without her marriage to John Rolfe and the resulting *Peace of Pocahontas*.

POCAHONTAS' PARENTS

On June 17, 1540, an Indian of the Pamunkey tribe named Wahunsenaca (sometimes Wahunsonacock) was born. As a young man he was made chief of a confederation of about five tribes. He later united approximately 31 Algonquian tribes in the Tidewater area (the

Chesapeake Bay and rivers that feed into it which experience tides) into the Tsenacomoco kingdom which we call the Powhatan confederacy. Wahunsenaca became their paramount chief, Chief Powhatan.

Wahunsenaca's first wife, his love wife, whom he married before he was made paramount chief, was from the Mattaponi tribe and was named Pocahontas. Over a period of approximately 20 years, she bore several children to Chief Powhatan. Their first child was a daughter named Mattachanna.

As the paramount chief, Wahunsenaca also had many alliance wives, young women from each of the 31 tribes who were married to him long enough to bear a child. They then returned to their village with the honor of having a child by the paramount chief, and married someone else. The alliance of tribes was solidified by having a blood relative of the paramount chief of the alliance present in each tribe.

BIRTH OF POCAHONTAS, SEPTEMBER 17, 1597

The last child of Chief Powhatan and his wife Pocahontas was born on September 17, 1597. She was named Matoaka, her private name. Matoaka means "flower between two streams."

Matoaka also was given the name Amonute for some purposes.

Although 1597 is the most frequent birth year the author has found, some historians and the U.S. National Park Service put Matoaka's birth in 1596. If that were true, Pocahontas would be a year older for all the events in this book. A few sources even use 1595 as the year of her birth which would make her two years older for all the events in this book.

Matoaka's mother Pocahontas died during the birth of her daughter Matoaka, who was later known as Pocahontas and is the subject of this book. Pocahontas reputedly means "playful" or "frisky." Matoaka's father sometimes called her Pocahontas. Later, during her Coming of Age ceremony when Matoaka could choose her own name to be known by, Matoaka chose to be called Pocahontas.

CHILDHOOD OF MATOAKA, POCAHONTAS

Matoaka was raised by her eldest full sister Mattachanna who was married to Uttamattamakin (sometimes called Tomocomo), a priest of the tribe. Matoaka had a number of older and grown brothers and sisters. Her brother Parahunt was chief of the Powhatan tribe. Her brother Pochins was chief of the Kecoughtan tribe.

Chapter 3: POCAHONTAS' HAD HER FIRST CONTACT WITH THE ENGLISH WHEN SHE WAS AGE 10

POCAHONTAS FIRST VISITED THE JAMESTOWN FORT AS A DIPLOMATIC ENVOY WHEN SHE WAS AGE 10

May 1608 was Pocahontas' first visit to the fort at Jamestown and her first known contact with the English. No Jamestown chronicler mentions her until that time. Pocahontas may have seen or met John Smith on that visit. Apparently she was at least seen by him.

On June 2, 1608, John Smith wrote a letter about Jamestown that was later published as *A True Relation of Such Occurrences and Accidents of Note as Have Happened in Virginia Since the First Planting of That Colony Which Is Now Resident in the South Part Thereof, Till the Last Return From Thence.* Smith told of his December 1607 capture by the Indians and being taken to Chief Powhatan. He made no mention of being attacked with clubs or of the presence of Pocahontas during his captivity.

Smith first mentioned Pocahontas in the same June 1608 letter in which he related his December 1607 capture. In April 1608, Smith captured seven Paspaheghan Indians as a result of a trade disagreement. The Paspaheghans were one of about 31 tribes in the Powhatan confederacy. Smith related that in May 1608, Chief Powhatan sent his daughter and a messenger named Rawhunt as diplomatic envoys to secure the release of the Paspaheghans held by the colonists. He described Pocahontas as a ten year old child:

> *Powhatan, understanding we detained certain Savages, sent his Daughter, a child of ten years old, which not only for feature, countenance, and proportion much exceedeth any of the rest of his people, but for wit and spirit the only Nonpareil of his Country. This he sent by his most trusty messenger, called Rawhunt, as much exceeding in deformity of person, but of a subtle wit and crafty understanding. He with a long circumstance told me how well Powhatan loved and respected me, and in that I should not doubt any way of his kindness, he had sent his child, which he most esteemed, to see me, a Deer and bread besides for a present ...*

POCAHONTAS VISITED JAMESTOWN AGAIN

As a child, Pocahontas returned to the Jamestown fort many times thereafter when her father sent gifts of food to the colonists. She was seen as a symbol of peace by the colonists. Pocahontas had stopped visiting Jamestown and the English settlers by sometime in 1610, the year of her first marriage, probably when she reached puberty.

Chapter 4: POCAHONTAS MARRIED INDIAN WARRIOR KOCOUM WHEN SHE WAS AGE 12

POCAHONTAS AND KOCOUM WERE MARRIED IN 1610

Pocahontas' first marriage was to a young warrior of the Potowomac tribe named Kocoum. He was one of about 50 warriors selected from the 31 tribes of the Powhatan nation to live in the village of Chief Powhatan and provide full time protection for him.

Pocahontas and Kocoum were married in 1610 when Pocahontas was likely 12 years old. They were probably married in the spring or summer, before her 13th birthday on September 17, although it is possible they were married after that.

After the marriage, they lived in Kocoum's home village, the Potowomac Indian village on the Potomac River. Before her marriage, probably when she reached puberty, Pocahontas had stopped visiting Jamestown and the English settlers.

In 1612, William Strachey, the Secretary of the Virginia colony, recorded in his The History of Travel into Virginia Britannia, that Powhatan had living 20 sons and 11 daughters *besides young Pocahontas, a daughter of his* [who sometimes came] *to our fort in times past, now married to a private Captain called Kocoum some 2 years since.*

So the colonists knew why the playful child Pocahontas had not been seen around Jamestown fort anymore even in peaceful times.

BIRTH OF POCAHONTAS' FIRST CHILD, LITTLE KOCOUM IN 1611

In 1611, Pocahontas gave birth to a son called Little Kocoum, named after his father, Kocoum, in the Potowomac village. Pocahontas, Kocoum, and Little Kocoum lived a normal Indian life in the Potowomac village for about two years. Then, suddenly, Pocahontas' world was turned upside down by the English.

CAPTAIN ARGALL WENT TO THE POTOWOMAC INDIAN VILLAGE

In early April 1613, Captain Samuel Argall went on a trading mission to the Potowomac village. Unknown to him, this is the village where

Pocahontas, her husband Kocoum, and their child Little Kocoum, lived. It had been about four years since Pocahontas had any interaction with the English settlers. She was 15 years old, having been born September 17, 1597.

CAPTAIN ARGALL DISCOVERED THAT POCAHONTAS LIVED IN POTOWOMAC

Chief Japazaw of the Potowomac village was Kocoum's older brother. By chance, Captain Argall learned that Pocahontas lived in the village. He threatened Chief Japazaw and his wife and got them to bring Pocahontas for a tour of his ship and to have lunch. Pocahontas was willing to take a tour of the English ship and went aboard the *Treasurer*.

CAPTAIN ARGALL'S ROLE IN VIRGINIA AND IN THE LIFE OF POCAHONTAS

Captain Samuel Argall first sailed to Virginia from England in May of 1609. The Virginia Company sent him on the *Mary and John* to find a shorter sailing route from England to Virginia which would avoid contact with Spanish ships. This required him to sail further north where it was thought the winds were unfavorable. He did, however, find a faster route, and returned to England with the news in October 1609.

In 1610, Captain Argall sailed to Virginia with Lord De La Warr, the new Governor who was needed because the Acting Governor Sir Thomas Gates was thought lost at sea. In fact, Gates' ship the *Sea Venture* had shipwrecked on Bermuda, where Gates and the others were marooned for nine and a half months. Gates and the others, including John Rolfe, built two small ships in Bermuda, the *Deliverance* and the *Patience*, and arrived at Jamestown on May 23, 1610. They found that conditions in Jamestown were so bad that most of the approximately 500 settlers of the previous autumn died and the colony was reduced to 60 people. That winter came to be called the "Starving Time."

Gates decided to abandon Jamestown and sail to England with the survivors. As Gates and the survivors, including John Rolfe, were sailing down the James River for England, they met Captain Argall and Lord De La Warr on the *De La Warr* at Mulberry Island in the James River on June 8, 1610. Lord De La Warr made them turn back. He had supplies that would feed them while they rebuilt Jamestown.

In March 1611, Captain Argall left Virginia for England with a sick Lord De La Warr. They landed in England in June 1611.

As we shall see, Captain Samuel Argall was an actor in several important moments in the life of

Pocahontas, and in the John Rolfe and Pocahontas saga.

Chapter 5: WHEN SHE WAS AGE 15, POCAHONTAS WAS KIDNAPPED AND HER HUSBAND KOCOUM WAS KILLED BY ENGLISH CAPTAIN SAMUEL ARGALL

CAPTAIN SAMUEL ARGALL KIDNAPPED POCAHONTAS

On September 17, 1612, Captain Samuel Argall arrived again in Virginia. It was during this trip that he took his ship the *Treasurer* on a trading visit to the Potowomac village where Pocahontas lived with her husband Kocoum and their child Little Kocoum.

On April 11, 1613, Captain Argall induced Chief Japazaw of the Potowomac tribe and his wife to bring Pocahontas on board his ship the *Treasurer*, ostensibly for a tour of the English ship and lunch. Chief Japazaw was the older brother of Pocahontas' husband, Kocoum.

After lunch on his ship, Captain Argall gave Chief Japazaw and his wife a copper kettle and sent them to shore. Captain Argall prevented Pocahontas from leaving his ship, kidnapping her. Pocahontas was 15 years old. Captain Argall then sent soldiers to the village to kill her husband Kocoum, which they did. Little Kocoum was saved by the women of the village and hidden in the forest.

Little Kocoum would have many descendents, including the famous American entertainer Wayne Newton.

CAPTAIN ARGALL HELD POCAHONTAS FOR RANSOM

Knowing Pocahontas to be Chief Powhatan's daughter, Captain Argall asked for ransom. He demanded the release of English prisoners held by paramount Chief Powhatan, Pocahontas' father, and the return of all English weapons that were acquired by the Indians over the years. Chief Japazaw sent messengers to Chief Powhatan. Two days later the messengers returned and reported that Chief Powhatan accepted the ransom terms and asked Captain Argall to sail his ship up the Pamunkey River to the village of Matchut to receive the ransom.

AFTER CHIEF POWHATAN AGREED TO THE RANSOM DEMANDS, CAPTAIN ARGALL RENEGED AND KEPT POCAHONTAS PRISONER

On April 13, 1613, after receiving a favorable answer to his ransom demands, Captain

Samuel Argall left the Potowomac village, but sailed to Jamestown rather than to meet Chief Powhatan and receive the ransom. After reaching Jamestown, Pocahontas was sent to the new village of Henrico, 55 miles upriver from Jamestown. Sir Thomas Dale, the Marshal, was headquartered in Henrico.

CAPTAIN SAMUEL ARGALL'S VERSION OF THE KIDNAPPING

Captain Argall wrote a letter to Master Nicholas Hawes in June 1613, about two months later, describing his version of events. It is somewhat self-serving. Argall left out the part about killing Pocahontas' husband. Captain Argall also claimed that Chief Japazaw was willing to betray his brother Kocoum by giving his brother's wife Pocahontas to the English, and also was willing to betray his paramount Chief Powhatan by giving Powhatan's favorite daughter Pocahontas to the English. And the price Captain Argall paid and Chief Japazaw received for this betrayal? Argall's continued friendship and love for Chief Japazaw and his people. It's hard to believe that there were not more serious threats involved.

So take Captain Argall's account with as many grains of salt as you wish.

Whilst I was in this business, I was told by certain Indians, my friends, that the Great Powhatan's Daughter Pocahontas was with the great King Potowomac, wither I presently repaired, resolving to possess myself of her by any stratagem that I could use, for the ransoming of so many Englishmen as were prisoners with Powhatan; as also to get such arms and tools, as he, and other Indians had got by murder and stealing from others of our Nation, with some quantity of corn, for the Colony's relief. So soon as I came to an anchor before the Town, I manned my boat and sent on shore for the King of Pastancie [Chief Ayapassus] and Ensign Swift (whom I had left as a pledge of our love and truce, the voyage before) who presently came and brought my pledge with him: whom after I had received, I brake the matter to this King, and told him, that if he did not betray Pocahontas into my hands, we would be no longer brothers nor friends. He alleged, that if he should undertake this business, then Powhatan would make war upon him and his people; but upon my promise, that I would join with him against him, he repaired presently to his brother, the great King of Potowomac [Chief Japazaw], who being made acquainted with the matter, called his Council together. And after some few hours deliberation, concluded rather to deliver her unto my hands, then lose my friendship, so presently, he betrayed her into my boat, herein I carried her aboard my ship. This done, an Indian was dispatched to Powhatan, to let him know, that I had taken his Daughter and if he would send home the Englishmen (whom he detained in slavery, with such arms and tools, as the Indians had gotten, and stolen) and also a great quantity of corn, that then he should have his daughter restored, otherwise not. This news much grieved this great King, yet, without delay, he returned the messenger with this answer. That he desired me to use his Daughter well, and bring my ship into his River, and there he would give me my demands: which being performed, I should deliver him his Daughter, and we should be friends.

Having received this answer, I presently departed from Potowomac, being the 13 of April, and repaired with all speed to Sir T. Gates, to know of him upon what condition he would conclude this peace, and what he would demand: to whom I also delivered my prisoner, towards whose ransom within few days, this King sent home seven of our men, who seemed to be very joyful for that they were freed from the slavery and fear of cruel murder, which they daily before lived in. They brought also three pieces [guns], one broad Axe, and a long whipsaw, and one canoe of corn. I being quit of my prisoner, went forward with the frigate which I had left at Point Comfort, and finished her.

POCAHONTAS CONVERTED TO CHRISTIANITY

Pocahontas was sent to the home of Reverend Alexander Whitaker to be instructed in Christianity. Whitaker, along with Governor Dale, was a devout Calvinist or Puritan, not an Anglican like Reverend Richard Bucke in Jamestown.

Reverend Whitaker had a church and about 100 acres fenced off with a parsonage called Rock Hall in Henrico. He served the churches in both Henrico and another settlement called Bermuda Hundred.

John Rolfe assisted Reverend Whitaker with Pocahontas' Christianity lessons. Rolfe had a plantation called Varina Farms in Henrico where he bred Trinidad and Orinoco tobaccos and raised the first successful commercial crop of tobacco. John Rolfe was a widower whose first child died on Bermuda in February 1610 and whose wife Sarah Hacker Rolfe died in May or June 1610 shortly after their arrival in Jamestown from Bermuda.

JOHN ROLFE FELL IN LOVE WITH POCAHONTAS

Over time, during the time they spent together on Christianity lessons, John Rolfe and Pocahontas fell in love. Rolfe wanted to marry Pocahontas, but he had a big problem. At that time, interracial marriage was, at the very least, frowned upon and, as a practical matter, prohibited. Of course there were some colonists living with native women, but they were not married. And Pocahontas was not yet a Christian and was considered to be of a pagan religion. What was an English gentleman to do?

Chapter 6: POCAHONTAS MARRIED JOHN ROLFE WHEN SHE WAS AGE 16 AND BEGAN THE *PEACE OF POCAHONTAS*

JOHN ROLFE SOUGHT GOVERNOR DALE'S CONSENT TO HIS INTERRACIAL MARRIAGE TO POCAHONTAS

John Rolfe wrote a very long letter to the colony's Governor, Sir Thomas Dale. He professed his love, not lust, for Pocahontas, and asked for permission to marry her. The text of his long letter, full of Christian fervor and much soul searching, survives, and is reproduced in the APPENDIX. It is very interesting and the author recommends it to you. The spellings have been modernized to make it more readable.

In his letter, Rolfe recognized the impediment of interracial marriage and argued that it would be good for all. Pocahontas would become a Christian and live in English society, while the colony would benefit by converting a pagan and having better relations with the natives. Plus he loved her very much.

Ralph Hamor, another colonist, in his letter *A True Discourse of the Present Estate of Virginia, and the Success of the Affairs There Till the 18 of*

June 1614, summarized Rolfe's situation in a simpler style:

> *Long before this time, a gentleman of approved behavior and honest carriage, Master John Rolfe, had been in love with Pocahontas and she with him ... made known to Sir Thomas Dale by a letter from him [Rolfe], whereby he entreated his advice and furtherance in his life, if so it seemed fit to him [Dale] for the good of the Plantation, and Pocahontas herself acquainted her brethren [her brothers] therewith.*

In spring 1614, Governor Dale consented to Rolfe's marriage to Pocahontas. Then Rolfe sought Chief Powhatan's consent to marry his daughter.

ROLFE SOUGHT CHIEF POWHATAN'S CONSENT TO MARRY POCAHONTAS

As part of John Rolfe's effort to secure the permission of Chief Powhatan for Rolfe to marry Pocahontas, Governor Dale sent Captain Samuel Argall and 150 men aboard the *Treasurer* up the York River seeking the Indians. In order to show a peaceful intent to this show of force, John Rolfe and Pocahontas were on board. Captain Samuel Argall was again part of the Pocahontas and John Rolfe story.

Captain Argall and his men met some resistance at the first Indian village they encountered, so they sacked and burned the village and killed five or six Indian men. Their actions seem inconsistent with a peaceful intent.

Farther upriver, at Werowocomoco, which in the early days of Jamestown had been paramount Chief Powhatan's village, the English went ashore with Pocahontas. She refused to speak to any Indians other than royalty. Shortly, two of her brothers came to speak with her. Pocahontas' brothers agreed to remain as hostages while John Rolfe and young Rob Sparkes sought Powhatan's permission for Rolfe to wed Pocahontas.

Chief Powhatan was three days journey away, so Rolfe met with Powhatan's younger brother Opechancanough (sometimes Opechankeno). A message was received from Powhatan. Chief Powhatan gave permission for the marriage of Pocahontas and John Rolfe, and Chief Powhatan further suggested a general peace between the natives and the settlers. This was more than the English settlers had expected.

Pocahontas' feelings toward John Rolfe were not recorded in writing. Rolfe's feelings toward her were set forth in his letter to Governor Dale. Pocahontas did speak with two of her brothers before her father agreed to let her marry Rolfe, so presumably if she had objected, her father, the paramount chief, wouldn't have agreed to the marriage. In addition to John Rolfe's writing, both Ralph Hamor, quoted above, and Governor Dale, quoted later, spoke of the love of Pocahontas and John Rolfe in their writings.

ENGAGED TO BE MARRIED

Rolfe was overjoyed. He and Pocahontas were now formally engaged. Governor Dale quickly accepted Chief Powhatan's offer of peace.

THE BAPTISM OF POCAHONTAS

Pocahontas was baptized as a Christian in early April 1614, by Reverend Alexander Whitaker who, along with John Rolfe, had instructed her in Christian teachings. The baptism probably took place in Whitaker's Henrico Puritan church, but perhaps in the Jamestown Anglican Church. The baptism was attended by John Rolfe, Governor Dale, and some of Pocahontas' Indian relatives. Pocahontas, who already had adopted English attire, was given the English name of Rebecca.

The Baptism of Pocahontas is commemorated in the United States Capitol building in Washington, D.C. A large painting, 18 feet wide by 12 feet high, of the imagined scene hangs in the rotunda of the building, one of eight similarly sized paintings of the history of the United States. It was commissioned in 1836 and installed in 1840. The painting is a testament to how important the period of peace that followed was to the survival of the colony and the establishment of the United States.

Also, in the 1800's, American settlers on the frontier had a lot of conflict with Indians. In addition, few Indians had been converted to Christianity in over 200 years of trying. Pocahontas' baptism represented the ideal that American government officials had for the way they wanted Indians to behave.

The event was further commemorated in 1870 when an engraving of the Baptism of Pocahontas painting appeared on the back of a $20 bill.

THE MARRIAGE OF POCAHONTAS AND JOHN ROLFE

Shortly after her baptism, Reverend Richard Bucke married Pocahontas and John Rolfe in the Anglican Church in Jamestown on April 5, 1614.

John Rolfe was a 28 year old widower, and Pocahontas was a 16 year old widow. Pocahontas' sister, Mattachanna, her husband the priest Uttamattamakin, and other Indians attended and witnessed the marriage. Governor Dale wrote that Pocahontas' uncle gave her away to Rolfe in the wedding ceremony.

In the summer of 2010, almost 400 years later, archeologists finally located the foundation of the Jamestown church the Rolfes were married in. The church was built in 1608 and was the second church built in Jamestown. The first church had burned down along with all the other buildings in a great fire on January 7, 1608.

In the summer of 2011, archeologists finished excavating the entire footprint of the 1608 church which was 24 feet by 60 feet. This is larger than the later 20 feet by 50 feet brick church which has now been reconstructed. It was much larger than any other building, and would have dominated the 1.1 acre fort.

THE FIRST INTERRACIAL CHURCH MARRIAGE IN AMERICA

John Rolfe and Pocahontas celebrated the first interracial church marriage in what would become the United States of America. The Rolfes started married life by living on Hog Island across the river from Jamestown, although some sources say they also lived on his Varina Farms plantation near Henrico.

Governor Dale said this about Pocahontas and her love for and marriage to John Rolfe in a letter from Jamestown dated June 18, 1614, to a friend in London:

> *Powhatan's daughter I caused to be carefully instructed in Christian religion, who after she had made some good progress therein, renounced publicly her country idolatry, openly confessed her Christian faith, was, as she desired, baptized, and is since married to an English Gentleman of good understanding, (as by his letter unto me containing the reasons for his marriage to her you may perceive) another knot to bind this peace the stronger. Her father and friends gave approbation to it, and her Uncle gave her to him in the church. She lives civilly and lovingly with him, and I trust will increase in goodness as the knowledge of God increaseth in her. She will go into England with me, and were it but the gaining of this one*

soul, I will think my time, toil, and present stay well spent.

THE *PEACE OF POCAHONTAS*

The *Peace of Pocahontas* began in 1614. It had been proposed by Chief Powhatan when he consented to Pocahontas' marriage to John Rolfe. It lasted for eight years until 1622. The *Peace of Pocahontas* was extremely important to the history of America. The Virginia colony now had a cash crop, tobacco, thanks to John Rolfe, to enable it to prosper financially. Yet, due to the effects of disease and frequent Indian attack, the colony had been unable to keep enough settlers alive to assure the colony's viability.

This period of peace allowed many more settlers to survive and allowed many more settlers to arrive from England. The English established a critical mass of colonists in Virginia so that the Indians couldn't force them out if the peace were to end.

John Rolfe had yet to learn the value to his tobacco crop of his marriage to Pocahontas. For Rolfe it was a love match. It was also an extremely important strategic alliance for the Virginia colony since it was the reason for the *Peace of Pocahontas*. And Rolfe's marriage alliance also would prove extremely important for his tobacco.

Chapter 7: POCAHONTAS' LIFE WITH JOHN ROLFE, HER ENGLISH VIRGINIA SETTLER HUSBAND

POCAHONTAS' RELATIVES, ROLFE'S FORMER ENEMIES, MENTORED HIM

John Rolfe came to Virginia as a settler, not an adventurer like most of his companions, with the desire to cultivate Caribbean tobacco, which was a milder variety than the native Virginian tobacco. It was this milder variety that was coveted in London.

Now that there was peace and John Rolfe was part of the family, Indians, probably Uttamattamakin, who was married to Pocahontas' oldest sister Mattachanna, and other priests who were in charge of curing the Indian tobacco, taught Rolfe how they cured tobacco. They hung individual tobacco leaves up to dry under cover from the weather, rather than piling them under hay to ferment as Rolfe did until then. This change in curing method in 1614 with help from his Indian friends resulted in John Rolfe producing exceptionally fine tobacco.

John Rolfe probably wasn't even looking for a mentor, as he was the most experienced farmer among the English, and the only one with knowledge of tobacco, his ambition. Yet Rolfe found a mentor in an unexpected place, from among his former enemies. It would have required a giant leap of faith for most Englishmen to listen to an Indian mentor, since most Englishmen considered the Indians to be savages. Yet because John Rolfe married Pocahontas, he was open to learning from her relatives. The Indian method of curing tobacco was radically different from the traditional English method. John Rolfe embraced this radical new idea and produced a superior tobacco leaf product.

A SON, THOMAS ROLFE, WAS BORN TO JOHN ROLFE AND POCAHONTAS

On January 30, 1615, a son was born to Pocahontas and John Rolfe, and they named him Thomas Rolfe. By coincidence, January 30 is also the author's birthday.

PROSPERITY

In 1615, the quantity of tobacco exported to England was 2,000 pounds. A cured tobacco leaf is very light in weight, so that's a lot of tobacco. This meant the beginning of true prosperity for John Rolfe and the colony. Rolfe's tobacco was extremely successful in England.

Chapter 8: POCAHONTAS BECAME THE TOAST OF LONDON WHEN SHE WAS AGE 18

THE MOST IMPORTANT WOMAN IN COLONIAL AMERICA, POCAHONTAS, AND AMERICA'S FIRST ENTREPRENEUR, JOHN ROLFE, WERE INVITED TO GO ON A PROMOTIONAL TOUR TO ENGLAND

In 1616, Governor Sir Thomas Dale asked John Rolfe and his wife Rebecca Rolfe, Pocahontas, to accompany him to London to help promote the colony and its tobacco crop. Even 400 years ago people appreciated that marketing was important and did promotional tours. Given Rolfe's experience on his only other ocean crossing in 1609, the tempest, shipwreck, and being marooned on a deserted island, it's a wonder Rolfe agreed to cross the Atlantic Ocean twice, first to England and then back to Virginia. Both John Rolfe and Pocahontas must have been very brave.

IN SEVEN YEARS, JOHN ROLFE CHANGED THE WORLD WITH POCAHONTAS' HELP

It had now been seven years since John Rolfe stepped onto the *Sea Venture* on May 15, 1609, and into his entrepreneurial adventure. In just seven years John Rolfe, with the help of Pocahontas, changed the world. The English were now successful in America both financially, thanks to Rolfe's tobacco, and in colonizing, thanks to John Rolfe's marriage to Pocahontas and the *Peace of Pocahontas*.

THE UNITED STATES IS ENGLISH SPEAKING AND OF ENGLISH HERITAGE

The territory that eventually became the United States of America now was a successful English colony, not a French, Spanish, or Dutch colony. So the United States has an English heritage with English common law and the English language. Pocahontas' marriage to John Rolfe and the resulting *Peace of Pocahontas* were critical to this development. Also, Rolfe founded an industry that provided America's biggest export for the next 150 years, and is a multi-billion dollar industry today, 400 years later, providing a strong economic base for the emerging nation.

Of course John Rolfe didn't live long enough to see all these effects of his entrepreneurial efforts. He even may not have realized that his actions had changed the world. Rolfe was a gentleman farmer with a strong goal which he achieved, and he pursued his love successfully, so he did have reason to feel very successful.

JOHN ROLFE SHARED HIS GOOD FORTUNE

Rolfe was personally generous. He shared his good fortune with other colonists who also planted his cross bred tobacco. In today's terms, he gave back to his community.

Rolfe's personal financial rewards were primarily grants of land and some profits from the sale of his tobacco. It's noteworthy that he shared his seeds and his curing process so everyone could thrive. As the colony grew and other settlers took up growing tobacco, even front yards in Jamestown were planted with tobacco.

TO ENGLAND WITH CAPTAIN ARGALL

In April 1616, John Rolfe, Pocahontas, their 14 month old son Thomas Rolfe, about a dozen Indians, and Sir Thomas Dale, sailed aboard the

Treasurer to England. The ship's captain was Captain Samuel Argall. That was the same ship and the same Captain who kidnapped Pocahontas three years earlier, on April 13, 1613. Pocahontas' oldest sister Mattachanna, who had raised Pocahontas, and her husband the priest Uttamattamakin were two of those who accompanied her to England. Also on board were 2,500 pounds of tobacco, about half of the amount exported to England in 1616.

SPANISH PRISONERS

Also on board the *Treasurer* were two Spanish prisoners, Captain Don Diego de Molina and his pilot Francis Lembry, who were captured in May 1611, nearly five years earlier. During the voyage, Lembry was discovered to be an Englishman working for the Spanish, and he was hanged as a traitor somewhere in the Atlantic.

ARRIVAL IN ENGLAND

On June 3, 1616, the *Treasurer* docked at Plymouth, England, over 200 miles from London. The Rolfes traveled by coach on the coach road to London. On June 12, 1616, Pocahontas, John Rolfe, and their son Thomas Rolfe reached London. Pocahontas' sister Mattachanna and her sister's husband the priest Uttamattamakin and ten other natives accompanied them.

HIGH SOCIETY

Sir Edwin Sandys, a Member of Parliament and a rising star in the Virginia Company of London, helped John and Rebecca Rolfe in London. They were invited and entertained by many titled and high society people.

THE FAMOUS SIMON VAN DE PASSE PORTRAIT

Later that year, Simon Van de Passe, a well-known engraver, was commissioned to engrave a portrait of Pocahontas and she sat for the portrait wearing English attire including an English hat. These engravings of her sold all over London and caused a popular sensation. Pocahontas was a celebrity in England.

AUDIENCE WITH THE QUEEN

In the fall of 1616, the Rolfes had an audience with Queen Anne. The couple and their Indian companions were celebrated throughout English society. Rolfe's success with tobacco was only exceeded by his wife's popularity.

TWELFTH NIGHT WITH KING JAMES I AND QUEEN ANNE

On January 6, 1617, Pocahontas and John Rolfe attended the Twelfth Night masque, or ball, given by King James I as guests of Queen Anne and the King. The play presented at the event was written by Ben Jonson and was called *The Vision of Delight*. It was quite an honor for gentleman John Rolfe, a successful entrepreneur, but not a nobleman, to be invited to the event and to meet the King. Yet the invitation was likely extended because Pocahontas was considered a Princess, the daughter of a King.

LONDON'S FOUL AIR

Understandably, Pocahontas and her Indian companions who had lived their whole lives in the clean forest air of Virginia didn't like the thick coal smoke which fouled London's air. So, in February 1617, the Rolfes moved from London to Brentford, a village about 9 miles north of London on the Thames River, where the air was cleaner.

RETURN TO VIRGINIA

The Rolfes decided it was time to go home to Virginia. In March 1617, John Rolfe,

Pocahontas, and the Indian party boarded the *Treasurer*, the same ship that had brought them to England and also the same ship which had been used to kidnap Pocahontas. The ship's captain was again Captain Samuel Argall, the same captain who had brought them to England and who had kidnapped Pocahontas in 1613. They sailed down the Thames River headed for Jamestown. Argall was in command of a three ship fleet, including the *George*.

Chapter 9: POCAHONTAS DIED WHEN SHE WAS AGE 19

POCAHONTAS, REBECCA ROLFE, PASSED ON

On March 21, 1617, Pocahontas took ill on board ship on the way down the Thames River. They landed the ship in Gravesend and took her to an inn. That day Pocahontas died in the inn at Gravesend, Kent, England, 25 miles downstream from London. Most historians think she died from tuberculosis or some other lung disease.

Pocahontas, who was born on September 17, 1597 and who died on March 21, 1617, was not yet 20 years old. She was survived by two children, Little Kocoum and Thomas Rolfe. They would provide Pocahontas with thousands of descendants. John Rolfe wrote in a letter of June 8, 1617, after his return to Virginia following her death, that Pocahontas said on her deathbed that all must die but it is enough that her child lives. That was a very mature and philosophical sentiment, especially for a 19 year old.

John Rolfe and Captain Argall and the *George* remained in Gravesend for Pocahontas' funeral which was held in St. George's Church, Gravesend, England. Pocahontas was buried in the vault beneath the chancel of the church. John Rolfe was once again a widower.

Meanwhile, the *Treasurer* went on to Plymouth, England, for final provisioning.

POISON?

The Mattaponi tribe of the Powhatan nation, the tribe of Pocahontas' mother, tells the story of Pocahontas' death differently. Their "sacred oral history" says that John Rolfe and Pocahontas were having dinner with Captain Samuel Argall in the Captain's cabin of the *Treasurer* on the first night of the voyage and Pocahontas became ill. When Pocahontas returned to her quarters, she felt sick in her stomach and vomited. Pocahontas told her sister Mattachanna that the English must have put something in her food. Mattachanna and her husband Uttamattamakin tried to take care of her. Pocahontas began to convulse and Mattachanna went to the Captain's cabin and got John Rolfe. By the time they returned to Pocahontas' quarters, she was dead. Back in Virginia, Mattachanna and Uttamattamakin told Chief Powhatan Wahunsenaca that Pocahontas was murdered in England, most likely poisoned.

TWO YEAR OLD THOMAS ROLFE STAYED BEHIND IN ENGLAND

When John Rolfe arrived in Plymouth, about 170 miles from Gravesend, with Captain Argall on the *George*, his son Thomas Rolfe was seriously ill. Thomas was just over two years old. John Rolfe was afraid the ocean voyage to Virginia would be too much for Thomas and could kill him. So John Rolfe left his son Thomas Rolfe with Sir Louis Stukely, the vice admiral for Devonshire, and arranged for Stukely to care for Thomas until John Rolfe's younger brother Henry Rolfe could come from London to get him. Henry Rolfe took care of and raised Thomas Rolfe. Imagine what John Rolfe must have felt when he had to leave his young son behind having just lost his beloved wife.

CHIEF POWHATAN RESIGNED AS PARAMOUNT CHIEF

Later in 1617 or in early 1618, Pocahontas' father Wahunsenaca, known as Chief Powhatan, turned over his position as paramount chief to his younger brother Opechancanough who was chief of the Pamunkey tribe, bypassing another brother Opitchapam who was older but considered weak and lacking in leadership ability. The new paramount chief Opechancanough had a reputation as a warrior.

POCAHONTAS' FATHER DIED

In April 1618, Wahunsenaca, formerly Chief Powhatan, died at age 78 (1540 to April 1618) within a year of Pocahontas's death. Some sources put his death in 1622, and some sources say he was almost 90 years old when he died, putting his birth some years earlier in 1535.

THE *PEACE OF POCAHONTAS* ENCOURAGED SETTLERS

In the next three years, from 1618 to 1621, the Virginia Company of London sent 50 ships and almost 4,000 men and women to Virginia as settlers. This compared with just 1,600 settlers sent to Virginia in the nine years from 1607 to 1616. The successful promotional tour of Pocahontas and John Rolfe must have encouraged this new enthusiasm, as intended.

JOHN ROLFE WAS A MEMBER OF THE FIRST LEGISLATIVE ASSEMBLY ON AMERICAN SOIL

John Rolfe, who had been appointed Secretary of the Virginia Colony in June 1614, was appointed as one of the initial members of the first legislative assembly on American soil, the Virginia

House of Burgesses, which met for the first time in Jamestown on July 30, 1619. The group was composed of Governor George Yeardley, six councilors including John Rolfe, and two representatives from each of the small settlements in the Tidewater region. They met in the choir of the church in Jamestown, the third church, the brick church which has now been reconstructed and can be visited in the Colonial National Historic Park in Jamestown.

Thus began the form of representative government that would evolve to shape the government of the United States of America. All this happened before the Massachusetts settlement of 1620 which, incidentally, was also sponsored by the Virginia Company of London.

JOHN ROLFE WAS ILL AND WROTE HIS WILL

On March 10, 1622, a Sunday, John Rolfe was ill and dictated his Will to his old friend Reverend Richard Bucke who had left England with him on the *Sea Venture* on May 15, 1609. Reverend Bucke transcribed Rolfe's Will, Rolfe signed it, and Reverend Bucke witnessed it. John Rolfe left property to his son Thomas Rolfe and to his third wife Jane and daughter Elizabeth Rolfe.

In 1619, John Rolfe had married for the third time to Jane Pierce. Rolfe was 34 years old, and Jane Pierce was 20 years old. Jane was a widow and the daughter of fellow colonists William and Joan Pierce. William Pierce had come over from England on the *Sea Venture* with Rolfe. His wife Joan Pierce and their daughter Jane, then 10 years old, had come to Virginia on the same voyage but on a different ship, the Blessing, arriving in Jamestown as scheduled in 1609. William Pierce and John Rolfe were among those shipwrecked on Bermuda in the *Sea Venture*. The Pierce mother and daughter were among the 60 who survived the "Starving Time" of the winter of 1609-1610.

John Rolfe had not seen his son Thomas since leaving him in England when Thomas was too ill to attempt the ocean crossing. John Rolfe never saw his son Thomas again.

THE END OF THE *PEACE OF POCAHONTAS*

On Friday, March 22, 1622, five years and a day after Pocahontas' death, Indians massacred 347 colonists and burned Henrico. That was approximately one-third of the colonists. The colonists in and around Jamestown and the John Rolfe family were safe, although some Native American sources suggest John Rolfe may have been killed that day. That was the end of the *Peace of Pocahontas*.

Chief Opechancanough was responsible for the massacre. He had decided it was time to rid Virginia of the English. It turned out to be too late to do that. The *Peace of Pocahontas* had enabled the English to get enough colonists in Virginia to withstand even this massacre.

JOHN ROLFE PASSES ON

In April 1622, John Rolfe died, most sources say, in Virginia. One source says he died while a passenger on the Neptune bound for England. He was 36 years old, about a month short of his 37th birthday on May 3.

Please note that in 2012 the County Records Office in Heacham, Norfolk, England noticed that the date of May 6, 1585 attributed to John Rolfe's christening was read incorrectly on the original church document in the Records Office's possession, and the correct date is May 3, 1585.

Later in 1622, John Rolfe's widow Jane Rolfe married again, to Captain Roger Smith. Elizabeth Rolfe, daughter of Jane and John Rolfe, was then raised in the Jane and Roger Smith household.

THOMAS ROLFE WENT TO VIRGINIA TO RECEIVE HIS LEGACY

Reportedly the English continually sought more land from the Powhatan Indians. Chief Opechancanough steadfastly replied that they would not give any more land to the English except to Pocahontas' son, Thomas Rolfe.

Thomas Rolfe went to Virginia in 1635 to claim his inheritance. He was 20 years old. Aside from taking possession of the land his father John Rolfe left him, Thomas Rolfe visited Chief Opechancanough and his Indian relatives and received a large tract of land that was set aside for him by Chief Powhatan because he was Pocahontas' son.

Appendix: JOHN ROLFE'S LETTER OF MARCH 1614 TO SIR THOMAS DALE, GOVERNOR OF VIRGINIA, SEEKING PERMISSION TO MARRY POCAHONTAS

HONORABLE SIR, AND MOST WORTHY GOVERNOR –

When your leisure shall best serve you to peruse these lines, I trust in God the beginning will not strike you into a greater admiration than the end will give you good content. It is a matter of no small moment concerning my own particular which here I impart to you, and which toucheth me so nearly as the tenderness of my salvation, howbeit, I freely subject myself to your grave and mature judgment, deliberation, approbation, and determination, assuring myself of your zealous admonitions and godly comforts – either persuading me to desist or encouraging me to persist therein with a religious fear and godly care, for which, from the very instant that this began to root itself within the secret bosom of my breast, my daily and earnest prayers have been, still are, and ever shall be poured forth with as sincere a godly zeal as I possibly may, to be directed, aided, and governed in all my thoughts, words, and deeds to the glory of God; and for my eternal consolation to persevere wherein I never had more need nor till now could ever imagine to have been moved with the like occasion.

But my case standing as it doth, what better worldly refuge can I here seek than to shelter myself under the safety of your favorable protection? And did not my cause proceed from an unspotted conscience, I should not dare to offer to your view and approved judgment these passions of my troubled soul, so full of fear and trembling is hypocrisy and dissimulation. But knowing my own innocence and godly fervor in the whole prosecution hereof, I doubt not of your benign acceptance and clement construction.

As for malicious depravers and turbulent spirits to whom nothing is tasteful but what pleaseth their unsavory palate, I pause not for them, being well assured in my persuasion by the often trial and proving of myself in my holiest meditations and prayers that I am called hereunto by the spirit of God; and it shall be sufficient for me to be protected by yourself in all virtuous and pious endeavors. And for my more happy proceeding herein, my daily oblations shall ever be addressed to bring to pass so good effects that yourself and all the world may truly say this is the work of God and it is marvelous in our eyes.

But to avoid tedious preambles and to come nearer the matter, first suffer me with your patience to sweep and make clean the way wherein I walk from all suspicions and doubts which may be covered therein, and faithfully to reveal unto you what should move me hereunto.

Let therefore this my well-advised protestation, which here I make between God and my own conscience, be a sufficient witness at the dreadful Day of Judgment (when the secret of all men's hearts shall be opened) to condemn me herein if my chiefest intent and purpose be not to strive with all my power of body and mind in the undertaking of so weighty a matter, no way led – so far forth as man's weakness may permit – with the unbridled desire of carnal affection, but for the good of this plantation, for the honor of our country, for the glory of God, for my own salvation, and for the converting to the true knowledge of God and Jesus Christ an unbelieving creature, namely Pocahontas, to whom my heart and best thoughts are and have a long time been so entangled and enthralled in so intricate a labyrinth, that I was even a-wearied to unwind myself there out. But Almighty God, who never faileth His that truly invocate His holy name, hath opened the gate and led me by the hand, that I might plainly see and discern the safe paths wherein to tread.

To you therefore, most noble sir, the patron and father of us in this country, do I utter the effects of this my settled and long conditioned affection – which hath made a mighty war in my meditations! And here I do truly relate to what issue this dangerous combat is come unto, wherein I have not only examined but thoroughly tried and pared my thoughts even to the quick before I could find any fit wholesome and apt applications to cure so dangerous an ulcer, I never failed to offer my daily and faithful prayers to God for His sacred and holy assistance. I forgot not to set before mine eyes the frailty of mankind, his proneness to evil, his indulgency of wicked thoughts, with many other imperfections wherein man is daily ensnared and oftentimes overthrown, and them compared to my present estate.

Nor was I ignorant of the heavy displeasure which Almighty God conceived against the sons of Levi and Israel for marrying strange wives, nor of the inconveniences which may thereby arise with other and like good motions, which made me look about warily and with good circumspection into the grounds and principal agitations which thus should provoke me to be in love with one whose education hath been rude, her manners barbarous, her generation accursed, and so discrepant in all nurtriture from myself that oftentimes with fear and trembling I have ended my private controversy with this: "Surely these are wicked instigations, hatched by him who seeketh and delighteth in man's destruction!" – and so with fervent prayers to be ever preserved from such diabolical assaults as I took those to be, I have taken some rest.

Thus, when I thought I had obtained my peace and quietness, behold, another but more gracious temptation hath made breaches into my holiest and strongest meditations, with which I have been put to a new trial in a stricter manner than the former. For besides the many passions and sufferings which I have daily, hourly – yea, and in my sleep endured, even awaking me to astonishment, taxing me with remissness and carelessness, refusing and neglecting to perform the duty of a good Christian, pulling me by the ear and crying, "Why dost not thou endeavor to make her a Christian?" And these have happened to my greater wonder even when she hath been furthest separated from me, which in common reason, were it not an undoubted work of God, might breed forgetfulness of a far more worthy creature.

Besides, I say the holy spirit of God hath often demanded of me why I was created if not for transitory pleasures and worldly vanities, but to labor in the Lord's vineyard, there to sow and plant, to nourish and increase the fruits thereof, daily adding with the good husband in the Gospel somewhat to the talent, that in the end the fruits may be reaped to the comfort of the laborer in this life and his salvation in the world to come. And if this be, as undoubtedly this is, the service of Jesus Christ requireth of his best servant, woe unto him that hath these instruments of piety offered and put into his hands and willfully despiseth to work with them; likewise adding hereunto her great appearance of love to me, her desire to be taught and instructed in the knowledge of God, her capableness of understanding, her aptness and willingness to receive any good impression, and also the spiritual (besides her own) incitements stirring me up hereunto.

What should I do? Shall I be of so untoward a disposition as to refuse to lead the blind into the right way? Shall I be so unnatural as not to give bread to the hungry? Or so uncharitable as not to cover the naked? Shall I despise to actuate these pious duties of a Christian? Shall the base fear of displeasing the world overpower and withhold me from revealing unto man these spiritual works of the Lord, which in my mediations and prayers I have daily made known unto Him? – God forbid! I assuredly trust He hath thus dealt with me for my eternal felicity and for His glory, and I hope so to be guided by His heavenly grace, that in the end by my faithful pains and Christian-like labor I shall attain to that blessed promise pronounced by that holy prophet Daniel unto the righteous that bring many unto the knowledge of God, namely, that they shall shine like the stars for ever and ever. A sweeter comfort cannot be to a true Christian, nor a greater encouragement for him to labor all the days of his life in the performance thereof, nor a greater gain of consolation to be desired at the hour of death and in the day of judgment.

Again, for the lawfulness of marriage, I hope I do not far err from the meaning of the holy Apostle that the unbelieving husband is sanctified by the believing wife, and the unbelieving wife by the believing husband, etc.; upon which place Mr. Calvin in his Institutions, lib. 4, cap. 16, sect. 6, sayeth, "Even as the children of the Jews were called a holy seed because being made heirs of the same covenant which the Lord made with Abraham they were different from the children of the ungodly, for the same reason even yet also the children of Christians are accounted holy, yea, although they be the issue but of one parent faithful, and, as the prophet witnesseth, they differ from the unclean seed of idolatry." And thus with my reading and conference with honest and religious persons have I received no small encouragement, besides *serena mea conscientia*, "the clearness of my conscience," clean from the filth of impurity, *quae est instar muri ahenei*, "which is unto me as a brazen wall." If I should set down at large the perturbations and godly motions which have striven within me in this my godly conflict, I should but make a tedious and unnecessary volume. But I doubt not these shall be sufficient both to certify you of my true intents in discharging of my duty to God and to yourself, to whose gracious providence I humbly submit myself, for His glory, your honor, our country's good, the benefit of this plantation, and for the converting of one unregenerate to regeneration – which I beseech God to grant for His dear son Christ Jesus His sake.

    Now if the vulgar sort, who square all men's actions by the base rule of their own filthiness, shall tax or taunt me in this my godly labor, let them know it is not any hungry appetite to gorge myself with incontinency. Sure, if I would and were so sensually inclined, I might satisfy such desire (though not without a seared conscience) yet with Christians more pleasing to the eye and less fearful in the offense unlawfully committed. Nor am I in so desperate an estate that I regard not what becometh of me, nor am I out of hope but one day to see my country, nor so void of friends, nor mean in birth but there to obtain a match to my great content, nor have I ignorantly passed over my hopes there, or regardlessly seek to lose the love of my friends by taking this course. I know them all and have not rashly overslipped any.

But shall it please God thus to dispose of me, which I earnestly desire to fulfill my ends before set down, I will heartily accept of it as a godly tax appointed me, and I will never cease – God assisting me – until I have accomplished and brought to perfection so holy a work, in which I will daily pray God to bless me to mine and her eternal happiness.

And thus desiring no longer to live to enjoy the blessings of God than this my resolution doth tend to such godly ends as are by me before declared, not doubting of your favorable acceptance, I take my leave, beseeching Almighty God to rain down upon you such plentitude of His heavenly graces as your heart can wish and desire, and so I rest.

At your command most willing to be disposed of, JOHN ROLFE.

OTHER BOOKS BY JOHN L. ROLFE

AMERICAN'S FIRST ENTREPRENEUR: How John Rolfe's Courage, Persistence, and Relationships Changed the World

PRINCESS BUTTERCUP THE CAT'S CROSS-COUNTRY ROAD TRIP #3, with Randy C. Rolfe

THE AFFIRMATIONS BOOK FOR SHARING, with Randy C. Rolfe

ABOUT THE AUTHOR
JOHN L. ROLFE

John L. Rolfe always knew that he was named for John Rolfe of Jamestown and Pocahontas fame. It was only after he retired as a Philadelphia lawyer that he researched the history of John Rolfe 400 years ago. The author discovered that the first permanent English colony in what would become the United States would not have succeeded without John Rolfe's entrepreneurial success in breeding and cultivating Caribbean tobacco. The history fascinated John L. Rolfe, and he wrote **AMERICA'S FIRST ENTREPRENEUR** about John Rolfe.

The author also discovered that the first permanent English colony would not have succeeded without John Rolfe's marriage to

Pocahontas and the resulting *Peace of Pocahontas*. John L. Rolfe realized that Pocahontas was the most important woman in colonial America. He discovered through talking with people that there was a lot of misinformation about Pocahontas, often caused by the many falsehoods in the animated films about Pocahontas. That led the author to write **POCAHONTAS AND HER TWO HUSBANDS: The TRUTH, Not Animated Fiction, About Kocoum and John Rolfe (Not John Smith)**.

John L. Rolfe is the father of two grown children. He lives with his first, only, and trophy wife in Pennsylvania. They also spend time at their vacation homes in California and Ontario. Rolfe enjoys reading, movies, classic and exotic cars, wine, Belgian Ales, craft beers, food, and travel. John L. Rolfe also loves to speak about John Rolfe and Pocahontas, and about entrepreneurship.

Printed in Great Britain
by Amazon